Amazing Life Lessons

Lessons from the Account of Joseph

Precious Chitwa

DEDICATION

I would like to dedicate this work to all who desire to know God and pursue a relationship with Him.

CONTENTS

ACKNOWLEDGMENTS

I would like to thank God for seeing this work through from its inception and it is my prayer that it may be a blessing to all who read it.
I would like to thank my family for their selflessness, unconditional love and support.
I would also like to thank my friends who have become my family, for their support and encouragement.
Furthermore, I would like to thank Dr. Sam Mahlangu, Mrs Patricshia Mahlangu and the rest of my Adventist Home Convivium family for their support and contribution to this work.
A special thanks to Angeline Edwards for her assistance and contribution to this work.

PREFACE

The account of Joseph has been one of my favourites since I first heard it in my kindergarten class as a child. I always desired to emulate his courage and faithfulness to God in my Christian walk. As I grew older, I got to experience the temptations that came with age which made me appreciate the experience of Joseph even more. With time, God rolled back the curtain of understanding for me concerning Joseph's account, and its relevance in my Christian walk, which I am privileged to be sharing with you in this devotional.

I extracted lessons from specific parts of the book of Genesis, from chapters 37 to 50, with the assumption that this devotional would be read as an aid alongside the Bible, in order to grasp the full details of this account. Each devotion has a Bible verse and a brief background of the segment as well as a lesson.

This devotional is ideal for even the busiest person, as each devotion has been written to deliver a lesson in but a few short minutes. That being said, my hope, as you continue through this devotional, is that the story of Joseph will leap off the page, as by God's grace it has done so vividly for me.

What's The Point?

"Joseph, being seventeen years old, was feeding the flock with his brothers. And the lad was with the sons of Bilhah and the sons of Zilpah, his father's wives; and Joseph brought a bad report of them to his father."

Genesis 37: 2 (NKJV)

It is interesting how this chapter starts off with Joseph giving a bad report of his brothers to his father. This can cause one to wonder: "Did he do this to gain favour from his father? Was he offended by his half-brothers? Was it because of sibling rivalry or was he just a young man of integrity who was offended by evil-doing?"

Well, whatever the reason was, Joseph was hated by his brothers for giving this bad report. We would expect that Joseph's integrity would earn him some kind of reward but unfortunately, it resulted in his being sold into slavery.

In our daily lives, like Joseph, we might feel offended when we see a wrong being done and even find it hard to ignore sometimes. It could be workmates expecting us to turn a blind eye to fraudulent activities that they are doing or discrimination taking place in our department at work and so on. Such and many other offences take place in the presence of people irrespective of their age, social class, or gender. But God expects us to be faithful even when our lives are at risk.

However, one might ask, "What is the point of being truthful if it will only get me into trouble or if I will not receive any reward for it?"

Of course, one might get a reward on some occasions for whistleblowing but on others, one might lose their job, their place in the family or social group, or even their life for doing what is right.

Well, the thing is, integrity for a Christian should come because of the Holy Spirit's converting work on the heart. It results from our heart's response to God's love and saving grace. Obedience to God's law which includes being truthful always has rewards beyond all the rewards the world has to offer, eternal life. It also glorifies God's name and brings a sense of inner peace and fulfilment.

Furthermore, there is no injustice that can ever be done to us because of living right that will exceed the injustice Jesus experienced for our sake. He did not have to come to earth, to live such a trying life and to die such a terrible death. But He did it anyway because He loves us and does not want heaven without us. What could be worth more than reciprocating such an amazing love? Let us therefore through the power of the Holy Spirit endeavour to be faithful to God every step of the way.

Who Do You Think You Are?

"And his brothers said to him, "Shall you indeed reign over us? Or shall you indeed have dominion over us?" So, they hated him even more for his dreams and for his words."

Genesis 37:8 (NKJV)

Sometimes I wonder, if Reuben had these dreams instead of Joseph, would it have been more acceptable to his family since he was the oldest son? Could it have been because of his age that his father and brothers were offended that Joseph had such dreams?

Well, what is evident about God in his dealings with man is that He is no respecter of man. God does not care about social class, age and skin colour. He simply assigns a spiritual gift or position to whom He desires and even equips that person for the achievement of that task or office. For instance, Josiah was only 8 when he began to reign as King. The Lord appointed him and the Bible says, *"He did what was right in the sight of God"*-2 Kings 22:1.

Another example is that of David whose own father did not think of presenting him to Samuel the prophet when he went to his house to anoint one of his sons as king. It seemed to him that David was not worthy of being anointed as king.

In the same way, when God reveals a course that we should pursue, the people in our lives including family members may murmur and cause us to think we do not fit the job description. Since they have known us for a long time, they may even discourage us by reminding us of our weaknesses and explaining so lovingly why we cannot fulfil that assignment that God has revealed to us. But we should not look within ourselves for the ability to fulfil God's will, for He qualifies those He calls. And if the work he assigns us to do requires finances, He will definitely take care of the bills. Therefore, whatever the assignment God gives you, do not like Moses say you stammer, or like Jeremiah that you are only a child but like Isaiah, say, *"Here I am; send me."*-Isaiah 6:8 (NLT)

Evils of Favouritism

"Come therefore, let us now kill him and cast him into some pit; and we shall say, 'Some wild beast has devoured him.' We shall see what will become of his dreams!"

Genesis 37:20 (NKJV)

Favouritism by its definition is the practice of giving unfair preferential treatment to one person or group at the expense of another. This preferential treatment could be based on skin colour, social status, gender, tribe and even the fact that that person is a relative. This might seem insignificant at first just as it seemed insignificant to Jacob when he made the coat of many colours for Joseph and favoured him more than his other children. Little did Jacob know that he was digging his own son's 'grave'. With time, the malignant cancer of jealousy rooted itself so deep in Joseph's brothers that the majority of them were willing to kill him without a second thought when the opportunity presented itself.

A typical example of what favouritism can result in is the Rwandan genocide. Generally, the Hutu-Tutsi strife stemmed from class warfare, with the Tutsis being perceived to have had greater wealth and social status (as well as favouring cattle ranching over what was seen as the lower-class farming of the Hutus). These class differences started during the 19th century, were exacerbated by colonization, and exploded into violence that left around 800, 000 Tutsis and moderate Hutus killed by the end of 3 months.[1]

I'm sure you must be thinking, "How could anyone in their right mind do such a thing?!"

However, according to Jeremiah 17:9, we are told, *"The heart is deceitful above all things, and desperately wicked: who can know it?"*

____

[1]History.com Editors, Rwandan Genocide, October 14, 2009, A & E Television Networks, Retrieved from https://www.history.com/topics/africa/rwandan-genocide

Only God knows the extent of our depravity. Left to ourselves, we are hopelessly wicked. It is therefore, very dangerous for us to entertain any evil thoughts as they have the potential of being acted out once the opportunity presents itself. Of course, it might not happen overnight but with time and the right conditions, even we would be shocked at what we can do.

Since we cannot control other people's actions towards us, it is also very important that we be careful not to cherish an unforgiving spirit regardless of what someone has done to us. This is because holding on to grudges is like holding hot coals in our hands. The tighter we hold on to the hot coals, the deeper they eat into our flesh and cause further damage. And so, instead of our wounds healing with time, they grow deeper and eat us up like cancer. Who knows then what we would do if the opportunity for revenge presented itself?

 Thankfully, not only is God able to help us forgive but He is also able to forgive our sins and cleanse us from all unrighteousness (1 John 1:9).

I like how Ezekiel 26:26 and 27 break this down. Here God says, *"I will give you a new heart and put a new spirit within you; I will take the heart of stone out of your flesh and give you a heart of flesh. I will put My Spirit within you and cause you to walk in My statutes, and you will keep My judgments and do them."*

Therefore, we should avoid favouritism at all costs and since we do not have the power to change the treatment that we receive from others, we have to the power to choose how we respond to that treatment. Instead of cherishing vengeance in our hearts, let us show love and mercy inste

Dreams

"Now Joseph had a dream, and he told it to his brothers, and they hated him even more."

Genesis 37:5 (NKJV)

Joseph had a dream in which he and his brothers and were binding sheaves in the field. He then noticed his sheaf rise and stand upright while the sheaves of his brothers stood all around him and bowed down to it. When he shared this with his brothers, they hated him even more because the dream implied that he would have dominion or reign over them.

The Bible continues to say, he had another dream and told it to his brothers, and said, "Look, I have dreamed another dream. And this time, the sun, the moon, and the eleven stars bowed down to me." This attracted a rebuke from his father who said to him, *"What is this dream that you have dreamed? Shall your mother and I and your brothers indeed come to bow down to the earth before you?"*-Genesis 37: 9, 10 (NKJV).

This response must have been hard for Joseph to take because he did not understand why he was having these dreams in the first place, and how they applied to him. And probably he had thought it best to share them with those close to him, perhaps he is hoping for some empathy, comfort and even advice, but all he received was mockery, rebuke and hatred.

Like Joseph, God may have placed something that He would like us to do in our hearts. He might have even shown us a glimpse of the role we would have to play in the process of Him achieving the plans He has for us as He has stated in Jeremiah 29:11, *"For I know the plans I have for you," declares the Lord, "plans to prosper you and not to harm you, plans to give you hope and a future."*(NIV)

However, when we share this revelation from God with others, they might look at us in unbelief and even mock us, and some might keep silent with the hope that we will get back to our senses while others may lovingly tell us it is not possible, or it does not make sense.

Getting back to Joseph, from chapter 41 onwards, we are able to understand what God was communicating to him in the dreams as we see his life unfold while in Egypt. The God that brought to pass the plans that He had for Joseph, is the same one whom we worship today. No one except He knows each one of us fully and has the power to give us the ability to achieve above and beyond what we can ever imagine. Therefore, we should not be too quick to share the dreams God places on our hearts without His guidance and we should not allow others to discourage us from achieving what God has planned out for us

Blind Judgement

"Then Judah took a wife for Er his firstborn, and her
name was Tamar. But Er, Judah's firstborn, was wicked in the sight
of the Lord, and the Lord killed him."

Genesis 38:6, 7 (NKJV)

Now, I know we are talking about Joseph in this book but allow me to follow the digression of the writer in Genesis 38: 1-26. I believe it was not by mistake that this account finds its place here. So, Judah marries and has children who instead of giving him grandchildren, die mysteriously. And from the look of things, Judah and his family begin to suspect Tamar of being responsible for this.

Tamar, on the other hand, had been through the trauma of being widowed twice. As if this was not enough, her in-laws suspected that she was responsible for the deaths of her husbands. It is not mentioned in the Bible if they actually confronted her about this but we know for sure that Judah was entertaining that thought. I can only imagine how the people in her community treated her during this period. How she must have been topping on the women's gossip list; how she might have been glanced at in an awkward way every time she would leave her house. Was she accorded the same respect by her family, friends and community as before she was first widowed? Well, whatever the case, I suspect that the people in her family and community talked even more when she was sent back home to her relatives so that she could wait for Judah's youngest son to grow up until he was old enough to marry her.

This however, never happened because Judah was afraid that his youngest son might face the same fate as his older brothers. Despite all of this, Tamar was still expected not to entertain any man or even get married. What a life she led, and yet she was innocent in all of this. Perhaps, if Judah had enquired of the Lord what was really happening, maybe things would have turned out differently for both Tamar and Judah, but we know how things turned out unfortunately.

Like Tamar, many people in various societies today have been stereotyped as a result of unfortunate events in their lives. Apart from being widowed, they could have 'strange' Illnesses like mental disorders, uncommon physical deformities, disabilities, having a different skin colour and so on. What is worse for them is that the biological and even church family that is supposed to embrace and comfort them joins in making theories about what really caused the situation they are in.

Perhaps Tamar's experience is teaching us a lesson here of how bad the outcome maybe if we do not take the step to embrace, pray with and comfort those in such circumstances.

Stubborn Faith

"So it was, as she spoke to Joseph day by day, that he did not heed her, to lie with her or to be with her."

Genesis 39:10 (NKJV)

Joseph's life at this point had completely turned around from being His father's favourite to being a slave with no rights in a heathen land. Life would never be the same for Joseph from this point onwards. However, he had clearly resolved to stay faithful to God in spite of his circumstances. And God gave evidence of His presence in Joseph's life by blessing him to such an extent that his master noticed the hand of God in his life! In fact, Potiphar, his master, decided to entrust everything that he owned to Joseph's care because of this. Even as Joseph saw the favour God had bestowed on him, he did not lay back and lazy around but worked in harmony with God by faithfully executing his duties. The Bible also mentions that Potiphar did not even know what he owned at some point which presented a very good opportunity for Joseph to steal from him but he did not.

However, as we read this account further, we discover that everything was going well for Joseph until Potiphar's wife happened. This woman tried to seduce Joseph on many occasions, but the Bible says, *"… he refused and said to his master's wife, 'Look, my master does not know what is with me in the house, and he has committed all that he has to my hand. There is no one greater in this house than I, nor has he kept back anything from me but you, because you are his wife. How then can I do this great wickedness, and sin against God?' "*.

Regardless, she still persisted in her request but Joseph ignored her every time because he had stubborn faith. Joseph was determined not to change his position on this subject in spite of good arguments or reasons to do so. For instance, one of his excuses would have been that he was only a slave and needed to protect himself by giving in to her wishes so that she would not put him into trouble with his master. The other argument would have been that he was a man and could only manage to resist her for so long before giving in. But even when he knew what would result from standing his ground, he consistently did so. Unfortunately, things did not go well for Joseph as he was moved from his position of trust to that of a prisoner. Speak of jumping from the frying pan to the fire.

Like Joseph, we might face temptations that if we gave into, everyone around us would understand because, after all, we are only human. But just as Joseph was stubborn in his faith, God expects us to do the same because He does not allow any temptation to come through to us that we cannot overcome through the strength He provides us with- used by 1 Corinthians 10:13 (NKJV).

Therefore, regardless of the temptations we might face or what we may go through, we too can have this stubborn faith by God's grace.

Be Still

"Then it came to pass, at the end of two full years, that Pharaoh had
a dream; and behold, he stood by the river."

Genesis 41:1 (NKJV)

For two full years, Joseph was in prison without being at fault. Joseph had to endure this experience without knowing if he would ever be released from prison, let alone lead a normal life. If ever he would be released from prison, would he be a slave to a good master or a cruel one? What else would he have to endure in the future? Would he ever see his family again?

The thing is, even if he was released from prison, the future did not seem promising for Joseph. He had nothing to look forward to. However, In spite of all the questions that Joseph might have had while in prison, he still remained faithful to God even when his future did not look so promising. Joseph faithfully performed his daily duties regardless of the uncertainty of his future. Though He did not understand what was happening to him and why he chose to trust in God and to stay faithful to Him.

What are you going through at the moment? Do you feel God has abandoned you? Do you feel the burdens you are carrying weighing heavily on you? Have you been praying and not seeing your desired answers to your prayers?

A famous hymn I like whose author was Katharina Amalia Dorothea von Schlegel comes to mind. It goes like this:

Be still my soul: the Lord is on thy side

Bear patiently the cross of grief or pain;

Leave to thy God to order and provide;

In every change, His faithful will remain.

Be still my soul: thy best, thy heavenly friend

Through thorny ways leads to a joyful end.

Be still my soul: thy God doth undertake

To guide the future as He has the past.

Thy hope, thy confidence let nothing shake;

All now mysterious shall be bright at last.

Be still my soul: the waves and winds still know

His voice who ruled them while He dwelt below.

Be still, my soul: the hour is hastening on

when we shall be forever with the Lord;

when disappointment, grief, and fear are gone,

sorrow forgot, love's purest joys restored.

Be still, my soul: when change and tears are past

all safe and blessed we shall meet at last.

Like Joseph, regardless of what you may be going through, allow God to give you peace as you stay faithful.

Kindness In All Seasons

"Now there was a young Hebrew man with us there, a servant of the captain of the guard. And we told him, and he interpreted our dreams for us; to each man, he interpreted according to his own dream."

Genesis 41:12 (NKJV)

While Joseph was in prison, Pharaoh's butler and baker were brought in for some offences that they had committed. One night, they both had dreams which left them puzzled as they did not know the meanings of these dreams. Joseph had every reason not to be interested in helping Pharaoh's Butler and Baker, when he saw them looking, puzzled that morning after they had their dreams. He could have simply focused on other things and ignored them, after all, they were not even his countrymen and what did he have to gain from them anyway.

Additionally, Joseph had enough sorrows of his own but instead of 'pity parting', he showed concern for those around him regardless of who they were. That day, Joseph took the time to patiently listen to the butler and the baker as they shared the dreams, they had the previous night and told them their meanings. Little did he know that God would use this good deed to uplift him from his current situation.

We may be facing various challenges in our lives and sometimes things may get so tough that we do not even feel like smiling or talking to anyone. Joseph here is inspiring us to avoid having our justifiable 'pity parties' and to focus on helping others. You see, by God's providence, we encounter other people who have various challenges and need a 'Joseph' to connect them to an omnipresent-loving God who is willing to intervene in their situation. Thus, God desires to work with Him as conduits of His blessings to those we meet. And guess what? The conduits still get blessings in the process as well! What a wonderful God we serve!

In The Fullness of Time

"Then Pharaoh sent and called Joseph, and they brought him quickly out of the dungeon; and he shaved, changed his clothing, and came to Pharaoh."

Genesis 41:14 (NKJV)

What a day this must have been for Joseph. The night before like many others had been the same ordinary one with no special expectations of what would happen the next day. But on this very day which seemed like an ordinary one, God visited Joseph in a special way. This visit, however, was not decided on the actual day or two nights before because God had planned it even before the birth of Joseph. This was the day that God had appointed to begin fulfilling the dreams that He had revealed to Joseph while in his father's house. It had seemed like his brothers had shattered the actualization of these dreams by selling Joseph into slavery but alas in the fullness of time, God stepped in to fulfil them.

We may sometimes think that God is like us. Of course, we were made in His image and likeness but in Isaiah 55:8, 9, we learn this: *"For My thoughts are not your thoughts, nor are your ways My ways," says the Lord. "For as the heavens are higher than the earth, so are My ways higher than your ways, and My thoughts than your thoughts."*

What an amazing revelation!

We also see this revealed to us when God was calling Jeremiah saying, *"Before I formed you in the womb, I knew you; Before you were born, I sanctified you; I ordained you a prophet to the nations."* Jeremiah 1:5. Like Jeremiah, Joseph's appointment was not by chance. It was in the fullness of time according to God's calendar that he was called into the presence of Pharaoh at that specific moment to solve that specific problem and in the process was set in the position of authority only junior to the pharaoh.

Today, God is saying, *"Can a woman forget her nursing child, and not have compassion on the son of her womb? Surely, they may forget, Yet I will not forget you."* Isaiah 49:15 (NIV).

Regardless of where you are in life and which part of the world you live in; your social class, skin colour and all, God loves you beyond what you will ever understand or imagine.

You are not here by mistake. He is saying to you, *"For I know the plans I have for you," declares the Lord, "plans to prosper you and not to harm you, plans to give you hope and a future"*-Jeremiah 29:11 (NIV).

Glory To Whom?

"And Pharaoh said to Joseph, "I have had a dream, and there is no one who can interpret it. But I have heard it said of you that you can understand a dream, to interpret it." So Joseph answered Pharaoh, saying, "It is not in me; God will give Pharaoh an answer of peace."

Genesis 41: 15,16 (NKJV)

Joseph had been given a rare gift by God. This spiritual gift was not something that was common to have thus it definitely made him special in the eyes of people. It is a type of gift that could lead people to worship you and give you gifts. I Imagine Joseph walking into the king's palace at that crucial moment with all the eyes of the magicians, wise men, and everyone else who was there at that time, on him. Furthermore, Joseph had the full attention of the man who was the highest authority in Egypt. And the fact that the highly respected magicians and wise men had failed to interpret the king's dream meant that Joseph would be regarded with respect above them by everyone in Egypt including the king himself if he managed to deliver. Joseph was aware of this and had the opportunity of a lifetime to bask in the glory and to earn their favour and everything else that would come along with it, but instead, he quickly directed all the attention to God.

Like Joseph, each one of us has been given one or more gifts by God. It may be that of singing, preaching, prophesying, and teaching, only to mention a few. Additionally, God may have blessed you with the ability to influence the people around you and with the advantage that social media avails to us today, we could influence people from different parts of the world as well. For others, it may be positions of influence because of the wealth, intelligence, eloquence, and other advantages that they possess. These gifts and blessings grant us various privileges including having people regard us highly. Since it is a human desire to be highly regarded, it is important not to give in to the temptation of receiving all the glory with the help of the Holy Spirit.

All glory belongs to God because He is the one who deserves all the praise. He is the one who gives us these gifts and all that we own. Even the things we claim to have worked so hard for, He is the one who gave us the strength, wisdom, and sanity to acquire them. He is omniscient, omnipotent, and omnipresent and yet He so humbly invites us to reason with Him- from Isaiah 1:18, and patiently tolerates us. Furthermore, for the mind-boggling love that He has demonstrated by giving us His son, Jesus to save us from eternal death (John 3:16) and what He continues to do for us, does He not deserve all the glory, honour and praise?

Therefore, when the temptation of exaltation comes your way, pass all the glory to God for He alone is worthy to receive it.

I know In Whom I Believe

"Then Joseph said to Pharaoh, "The dreams of Pharaoh are one; God has shown Pharaoh what He is about to do".

Genesis 41:25 (NKJV)

I admire the faith of Joseph. It reflects the kind of relationship that he had with God. The Bible has not given us a detailed background of Joseph's gift of interpreting dreams while he was with his family back home or evidence of it before he was thrown into prison. Therefore, it leaves little room for us to assess how much practice Joseph could have had with this gift in order to be so sure that he would manage to interpret the dream of the Pharaoh at this point; as it is said, perfect practice makes perfect.

However, Joseph expresses his faith in God's ability to reveal the dreams that Pharaoh had the night before and their interpretation to him. Joseph confidently stood before one who could order his head to be cut off without hesitation with the claim that his God, whom Pharaoh and his subject knew nothing about, was showing Pharaoh what he was about to do. Joseph's life was on the line here and yet he confidently was about to deliver the message that God would reveal to him. He believed that God would use him once again, and He did!

In life, we may encounter situations where the outcome of trusting and obeying God would bring an end like that of Abel or of Joseph. However, one thing is for sure, God is faithful and every decision He makes is always for our eternal best.

The question for you and I to reflect on here would be, "Do you know in whom you believe, and do you have confidence in Him when faced with a challenge?

It Is Established

"And the dream was repeated to Pharaoh twice because
the thing is established by God, and God will shortly bring it to
pass."

Genesis 41:32 (NKJV)

In this context, I would like to believe that the word establish is being used to mean, to set up on a firm or permanent basis. In short, the above bible text is implying that God repeated the dream to Pharaoh twice because He had made a firm decision concerning what He would shortly bring to pass. And therefore, what God was simply communicating here is that He had made the decision and there was nothing that Pharaoh, his wise men, his sorcerers, or his gods could do to reverse it. God had made the decision and it was final.

What a demonstration of authority and power this was. Furthermore, this bible passage also indicates that God had decided to create this circumstance. I hope you get this clearly. What I am trying to say here is that God was not making use of an already existing circumstance in order to glorify His name but rather, He created this circumstance from scratch to glorify His name. And it is through this circumstance that he elevated Joseph to a position of authority in Egypt and gave him the assignment he had been preparing for.

If this is the God we serve, a God who creates a circumstance to glorify His name and uplift His servant, why then should we be anxious and fearful about tomorrow? Is there anything too hard for the Lord to do?

In Matthew 6:25-27, Jesus tells us, *"Do not worry about your life, what you will eat or what you will drink; nor about your body, what you will put on. Is not life more than food and the body more than clothing? Look at the birds of the air, for they neither sow nor reap nor gather into barns; yet your heavenly Father feeds them. Are you not of more value than they? Which of you by worrying can add one cubit to his stature?"*

Furthermore, the Bible says, *"Fear not, for I am with you; Be not dismayed, for I am your God. I will strengthen you; Yes, I will help you. I will uphold you with My righteous right hand"*- Isaiah 41:10 (NKJV).

Like Joseph, we might have been through the worst experiences in life, not knowing what the next minute of our lives holds. But we should never forget that the God who created the circumstance through which He blessed Joseph is always with us.

What Is Your 'Content'?

"And Pharaoh said to his servants, "Can we find such a one as this, a man in whom is the Spirit of God?"

Genesis 41:38 (NKJV)

I had heard the story of Joseph many times in my childhood, but I had never gotten this part until much later when I read it for myself. Before, I had what impressed the king was Joseph's ability to interpret his dreams. But as I got to this point in the scriptures where Pharaoh expressed why he thought Joseph should be put in that high position of authority, then I understood. Pharaoh gave that position to Joseph because it was, he in whom the Spirit of God was. That is what made him unique. A heathen king was able to see and perceive the presence of the Holy Spirit in Joseph and that is what made all the difference.

In Romans 8:9, 14, the Bible says, *"But you are not in the flesh but in the Spirit, if indeed the Spirit of God dwells in you. Now if anyone does not have the Spirit of Christ, he is not His. For as many as are led by the Spirit of God, these are sons of God."*

To drive my point home, let me share an analogy that I learnt from the first president of the Adventist Home Convivium, Broglio Laing, with you.

Have you ever noticed that when a glass is filled with water, we call it a glass of water? And when we fill it with milk, we call it a glass of milk? If we drink that milk and later fill it with orange juice, we call it a glass of orange juice. What we do is that we identify the glass by its contents. In the same way, like the glass, when we are filled with the Holy Spirit, people can tell that we are the sons and daughters of God or Christians. By our way of living and how we treat others. But if we do not have the Holy Spirit living in us then, since there are only two camps, God's camp and the devil's camp, we automatically are identified as being part of the devil's camp.

Notice that, just as the glass does not tell us what it contains but we see it for ourselves, in the same way, people will be able to tell who lives in us by looking at how we lead our lives.

Let us then sincerely ask for the Holy Spirit to come into our hearts and transform us so that we may be correctly identified as Christian, glasses full of the Holy Spirit.

It Shall Come To Pass

"Then the seven years of plenty which were in the land of Egypt ended, and the seven years of famine began to come, as Joseph had said. The famine was in all lands, but in all the land of Egypt, there was bread."

Genesis 41:53, 54 (NKJV)

I would like to think that at some point during the seven long years of plenty, some Egyptians could have wondered if truly the interpretation of the King's dream had been accurate. I can only imagine how many people were waiting to confirm if Joseph's interpretation of Pharaoh's dream was true. Apart from the Egyptians, people from the surrounding nations must have gotten wind of Pharaoh's plan of storing food consistently for a whole seven years. This had never happened in Egypt before. How could such a powerful nation like Egypt experience drought? And not for one or two but seven long years?

Well, regardless of what anyone might have thought, what God said would happen, came to pass.

The Bible is full of testimonies of how God dealt with men. It is these interactions that have given us more understanding of God's character and one character trait that is so pronounced is that God keeps His word. His word is true and whatever He says comes to pass. In Numbers 23:19, the Bible says, *"God is not man, that He should lie; neither the son of man that He should repent: hath He said, and shall he not do it? Or hath He spoken, and shall He not make it good?"*

Therefore, we should not doubt God's promises to us for He who has promised is faithful. One of my favourite promises that encourages me as I journey in this world is that of an event which God has promised will soon come to pass, the second coming of Jesus Christ. In Revelation 22:12, the writer narrates the words of Jesus saying, *"Behold, I am coming quickly, and my reward is with Me, to give to everyone according to his work"*- Revelation 22:12 (NKJV).

Whether or not we doubt this word like the people in the time of Joseph might have, it will l come to pass. Therefore, let us make things right with God as we look forward to the fulfilment of this promise.

Change With Time

"Then he took servings to them from before him, but Benjamin's serving was five times as much as any of theirs. So, they drank and were merry with him."

Genesis 43:34 (NKJV)

When Jacob heard that there was grain in Egypt, he sent his sons to go and buy some since their food was almost running out because of the drought. It was at this point that Joseph came face to face with his brothers since the time that they had sold him into slavery. As they arrived, his brothers bowed without knowing that they were fulfilling the very dreams they had despised which he had shared with them when he was young. Joseph pretends not to have recognized them and accused them of being spies with the intention of making them bring his young brother Benjamin to him. At this point, not knowing that Joseph could understand their language since he had been using an interpreter to communicate with them, his brothers began to accuse each other concerning what they had done to Joseph. With their feelings of guilt, they believed God was somehow punishing them for selling Joseph into slavery. And so, while holding onto Simeon in prison, Joseph allowed the rest of his brothers to return home with the instruction of bringing their youngest brother Benjamin.

When the brothers arrived, they narrated their experience and Joseph's command to their father which brought great stress to him. It was only because of the depletion of the food of the family and the persuasion of Judah that Jacob allowed them to return to Egypt with Benjamin, his youngest son.

Now, getting back to the bible text, we see Joseph testing his brothers by giving Benjamin a serving of food five times more than that of his elder brothers. To Joseph's surprise, none of them showed any sign of jealousy towards Benjamin. Clearly, something had changed. The men that Joseph knew when he was growing up were not the ones seated at the meal table in his house that day. What Joseph did not know was that with time, his elder brothers had learnt that the satisfaction which they had derived from selling him was short-lived. All they were left with was guilt resulting from what they had done to him all those years back. What if they had killed Joseph? Would they have lived with that? Only God knows.

This is one of the reasons why vengeance should be left to God regardless of how we feel when we are mistreated or hurt. This is because with time we are likely to realize that revenge never soothes the pain that has been caused to us or brings us back what we lost in the process. It might only make our situation worse. What we need to understand is that we live in a sinful world where no one is perfect and therefore, anyone has the potential of hurting us deeply, be it our loved ones or strangers.

Therefore, we should never cherish an unforgiving spirit or a spirit of revenge but always 'budget' to forgive others as God does for us. You may ask, what if the person who wronged me does not ask for my forgiveness? What if he or she is not remorseful and is undeserving of my forgiveness?

Let me ask you this: Did Jesus die for you while you were in sin or after you had given your life to him? The Bible says, *"But God demonstrates His own love toward us, in that while we were still sinners, Christ died for us"-* Romans 5:8. Come to think of it, we ask God for forgiveness more times than we can count because we sin every day.

We should also keep in mind that we are prone to making mistakes and offending others since we are not perfect, and this should lead us to be humble and forgive others because we will need that forgiveness sooner or later.

Of course, it is not easy to forgive but with God's help, it is possible, for all things are possible with God.

Think

"With whomever of your servants it is found, let him die, and we also will be my lord's slaves." And he said, "Now also let it be according to your words; he with whom it is found shall be my slave, and you shall be blameless."

Genesis 44:9, 10 (NKJV)

After the brothers had finished with their meal and were scheduled to leave the next day, Joseph thought of another test for them. Early in the morning on the day of their travel as they were preparing to leave, Joseph told the steward of his house to fill the sacks of each one of his brothers with grain and to place their money at the mouth of their sacks. For Benjamin however, his sack was to not only be filled with grain and money but also with Joseph's silver cup. And all was done according to Joseph's instruction.

After his brothers had started off, Joseph told his steward to follow them and ask them why they had repaid him with evil for good by stealing his silver cup. To this accusation, the brothers responded by saying, *"With whomever of your servants it is found, let him die, and we also will be my lord's slaves." And Joseph's servant responded to them saying, "Now also let it be according to your words; he with whom it is found shall be my slave, and you shall be blameless"*—Genesis 44:9, 10. Then each of them quickly let down his sack to the ground and opened it.

After the search, to the brothers' shock, the cup was found in Benjamin's sack. Can you imagine for a minute if Joseph was not the person, they were dealing with at that moment how things would have played out? What grave consequences they would have had to face for speaking without thinking through first?

Does this sound familiar? Have you had an experience where you wish you had thought through your words before speaking to them?

In Proverbs 21:23, the Bible says, *"Whoever guards his mouth and tongue keeps his soul from troubles."* Therefore, be wise. Don't be in a rush, think, then speak.

God's Plan

"And God sent me before you to preserve a posterity for you in the earth, and to save your lives by a great deliverance."

Genesis 45:7 (NKJV)

Joseph had been in the dark concerning God's plan for his life. He almost died at his own brothers' hands who by God's grace changed their minds and sold him into slavery instead. This path then led him to Potiphar, his master. While in Potiphar's house, his master's wife caused him to be sent to jail where he did not deserve to go. Later he met the king's butler who promised to speak on his behalf to the king. And because the butler forgot all about his promise to Joseph, he had to stay in prison for two more years before he was set free. One can only imagine how dark and hopeless Joseph's world was during this time. What is worth noting however is how he stayed faithful while he moved through this tunnel with no sign of any light except for God's tokens of favour in his life. Of course, the king's butler had brought him some light for a period of time until Joseph realized that he had been forgotten. But through all this darkness, Joseph held on tightly to God's hand not knowing what each day would bring. Furthermore, Joseph faithfully and consistently served God even when all hope was out of sight.

Coming back to the Bible verse written above, by this time, Joseph's life had totally changed with his new position of authority in Egypt, but the scars of his experiences remained. At this point, Joseph had every right to be bitter and aggressive with his brothers after all they had put him through. Who would have judged him if he had avenged himself for the horrible treatment that they had given him from his childhood to the things he had to go through in a foreign land which resulted from him being sold into slavery? It came as shock to his brothers when, instead of avenging himself, he made this statement instead: "God sent me before you to preserve a posterity for you in the earth, and to save your lives by a great deliverance." What manner of man does this?

It takes the Holy Spirit to work on one's heart to forgive and to choose to appreciate and focus on how God had turned a bad situation into a good one especially if that situation was deliberately caused by family, friends, church mates or enemies. But like Joseph, let us choose to focus on the big picture-God's plans for our lives and not the negative experience. We should appreciate the fact that God will always be there for us and will work all things for our good.

There Will I Nourish You

"There I will provide for you, lest you and your household, and all that you have, come to poverty; for there are still five years of famine."

Genesis 45:11 (NKJV)

From reading the account of Joseph, we can safely deduce that neither Jacob nor Joseph's brothers believed that Joseph would ever be in a position where they would look up to him for the sustenance of their lives and that of their households and livestock. In fact, the very thought of making obeisance to Joseph drove his brothers mad with fury earlier when Joseph had shared his dreams with them. However, at this point according to God's design, Joseph was placed in a position where they had to look up to him to take care of them which he so lovingly did.

In the place where I come from, the Copperbelt province of Zambia, we have this colloquial Bemba saying, "Akachalo kalitaila." The direct translation of this is, "the world is a tire". The implication of this statement is that the change that happens in this world can be likened to that the exchange of the positions of the top and bottom parts of a tire when a vehicle is in motion. As it moves, the part of the vehicle's tire that was at the bottom finds itself at the top while the one that was at the top touches the ground. In the same way, a person holding power and having influence today might not have it tomorrow. Similarly, a person having certain privileges today might lose them tomorrow. Therefore, it is important to treat others with respect and kindness.

I remember watching a video on Facebook in which the former Spokesperson of the Ugandan Government, Robert Kabushenga narrated his humbling experience after resigning as CEO of Uganda's biggest media conglomerate, New Vision Uganda. This listed company would publish at least 10 newspaper titles and operate three television stations and six radio stations in Uganda. There, he ran the show for 15 years until he resigned. After this, the reality of commonality began to sink in. It was his turn to have the unfamiliar short end of the stick; to seek others and not to be sought. To walk in and not be recognized, or even be turned away. It was his turn to lack, which he never foresaw or imagined. He had to depend on his wife financially when he had been the breadwinner all throughout. The main lessons that he mentioned to have learnt at this point were that money disappears and power is transient. And so, it is very important to treat everyone with kindness and respect for they are human too and are made in the image and likeness of God. However, let not your motive be about treating others well so that they can treat you well also when they are in a position of power but rather, do all these things as a response to God's loving kindness towards you without any expectations from those you show your kindness to.

Keeping Priorities in Check

"So He said, "I am God, the God of your father; do not fear to go down to Egypt, for I will make of you a great nation there. I will go down with you to Egypt, and I will also surely bring you up again, and Joseph will put his hand on your eyes."

Genesis 46:3, 4 (NKJV)

After his experience of being a fugitive, away from the homely comfort and favour of his parents, Jacob had come to appreciate the presence of God in his life. For it was the Lord who had comforted him on his way to his uncle Laban's house and it is He who had blessed him with wealth despite Laban's mistreatment. Furthermore, God touched the heart of Esau in Jacob's favour as he returned home so Esau changed his plans of killing him as he was on his way with his family, workers, and animals. Because of the relationship that he had built with God, Jacob ceased to make any move without the Lord's permission or approval.

After Jacob had received the true narration of what had happened to Joseph, his favourite son, it must have been a bitter-sweet moment for him. He must have been heartbroken and felt betrayed thinking back on how he had lived with the sorrow of having lost his son to a violent death. Then on this day, he was told that it had all been a lie. It must have been also sweet in that his son Joseph was still alive and waiting to see him. It was as if the Lord had called forth his son from the tomb after having buried him for a long time. But what was surprising was that Jacob wanted to hear from first God before taking any step toward Egypt. Even when it was clear that his family would no longer have to endure the drought and he would finally be with Joseph, his beloved son.

After receiving the Lord's blessing and assurance of being with him every step of the way, Jacob made sacrifices to the Lord and was on his way.

In our lives, every single day presents us with decisions for us to make. Decisions concerning what to wear; what to eat; where to work; what career path to take; whom to marry, and the list goes on. In how we make these decisions, we express who has control of our lives. Is it ourselves, our family, our friends, our church pastors, our employers, or God? Who do we consider as a priority in every decision that we make?

Let us take a lesson from Jacob by making God our priority in every decision we make.

Reap What You Sow

"Unstable as water, you shall not excel, because you went up to your father's bed; then you defiled it- He went up to my couch."

Genesis 49:4 (NKJV)

While on his deathbed, Jacob called all his sons to gather around him so that he could tell them about their future. Now as his children waited to receive his last blessing the Spirit of Inspiration rested upon him, and before him, in prophetic vision, the future of his descendants was unfolded. One after another the names of his sons were mentioned, the character of each was described, and the future history of the tribes was briefly foretold. Reuben is the firstborn and was the first in line.[2]

"Reuben, you are my firstborn, my might and the beginning of my strength, the excellency of dignity and excellency of power. Unstable as water, you shall not excel, because you went up to your father's bed; then you defiled it-He went up to my couch." – Genesis 49:3, 4

I can only imagine what a blow this must have been for Reuben. At this point in his life, he was settled and flourishing with his family in Egypt, and so much time had passed that he must have thought he had gotten away with his sin. Of course, he had been forgiven but on the day he least expected, he was informed by his dying father what the consequences of his sin would be.

At times, like Reuben, despite knowing what we ought to do, we make decisions to fulfil our pleasures and hope to get away with them, and sometimes we think we do. However, the truth of the matter is that the consequences will always catch up with us sooner or later as we are told in Galatians 6:7, which says, *"Do not be deceived, God is not mocked; for whatever a man sows, that he will also reap."* (NKJV)

Therefore, let us make our decisions with care having in mind that we will always reap what we sow.

---

[2] Patriarchs and Prophets, Joseph and His Brothers, Ellen G. White Writings, Retrieved from https://m.egwwritings.org/en/book/84.945#945

Carry My Bones

"Then Joseph took an oath from the children of Israel, saying, "God will surely visit you, and you shall carry up my bones from here."

Genesis 50:25 (NKJV)

As Joseph was nearing his death, he decided to take an oath from the children of Israel to carry his bones out of Egypt into the land that God had promised their forefather, Abraham. One of the definitions of an oath is that it is a solemn promise, often invoking a divine witness, regarding one's future action or behaviour. In the time of Joseph, oaths were taken to certify the truth of an utterance and to pledge fidelity to one's word. Oaths were employed both in judicial matters and in a variety of everyday affairs and were made by those involved to assure the other party or parties of their trustworthiness as they were tangible signs by which the authenticity of their promises was guaranteed. Furthermore, in taking an oath or vow in God's name, they were saying that their word was so truthful that they were willing to suffer the judgment of God if they broke it. On a divine level, however, God would swear oaths not because He was untrustworthy, rather, He swore oaths as a condescension to them, to give them help in trusting His promises.

Therefore, for Joseph to have taken an oath from the children of Israel instead of just leaving them an instruction to carry his bones when God took them out of Egypt, shows that he believed with all of his being that God would keep His word. And I would like to believe this oath became an encouragement to the children of Israel after Joseph had died while they suffered in bondage. Probably every time they would feel defeated, they would remember the bones of Joseph as a sign of his faith in how God would fulfil His promise of rescuing them and making them a great nation. The bones of Joseph to them stood as a testimony of the word that God had promised to fulfil.

As for us today, Jesus has said, *"Let not your heart be troubled; you believe in God and in Me. In My Father's house are many mansions; if it were not so, I would have told you. I go to prepare a place for you. And if I go and prepare a place for you, I will come again and receive you to Myself; that where I am, there you may be also."* John 14:1-3

The question here is, what evidence are we giving to our family, friends, community, workmates, strangers and others that Jesus will return and take us home? Joseph made a very strong statement by taking an oath from the children of Israel to show that he believed God's word with all his heart. His actions spoke the loudest.

What are our actions speaking to those around us today? And if you and I were to die today, would anyone be encouraged by the faith that we would have shown in the second coming of Jesus Christ when they feel defeated by the troubles of this world?

CONCLUSION

As we navigate through life, making decisions that yield good results is not something that comes naturally. And regardless of how much wisdom and experience we may have; the fruits of our decisions are not always sweet but sour and bitter at times. For this reason, God gave us His scriptures out of His love for us so that we may tap into His infinite wisdom to safely navigate this life.

In 2 Timothy 3:16, 17, the Bible says, *"All Scripture is given by inspiration of God, and is profitable for doctrine, for reproof, for correction, for instruction in righteousness, that the man of God may be complete, thoroughly equipped for every good work."* (NKJV)

It is therefore my desire and prayer that these amazing life lessons that I have shared with you from the account of Joseph will achieve the purpose of scripture in your life today.

PRECIOUS CHITWA

Precious Chitwa is an Economist who also freelances as a content writer and editor. She also serves as a literature evangelist and likes to read, write, bake and take walks in nature. Her passion for healthy living and desire to help others with their health led her to also attain a Certificate in Lifestyle Education.

Precious is passionate about sharing knowledge and insights to help others grow in their faith. She started her journey in evangelism by sharing devotions at church youth meetings and vespers and sharing voice notes of her exciting discoveries as she studied the Bible with friends and family.

She was inspired to write this devotional on the account of Joseph after having a spiritually uplifting experience during her low moments in her Christian walk as she prayerfully read it word for word. It is her hope and prayer that her readers will find comfort, inspiration, and guidance through these daily reflections.

Connect with Precious Chitwa on LinkedIn, Instagram and Facebook

https://www.instagram.com/preciouschitwa

Also, can send a message to email:

PRECIOUSBOOKS07@GMAIL.COM